A FATHER'S
LITTLE INSTRUCTION BOOK

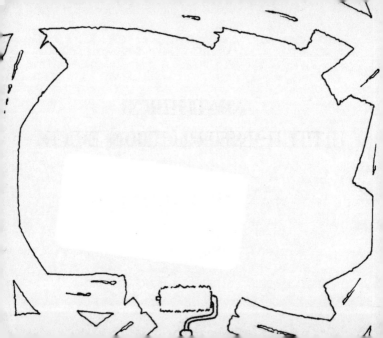

A FATHER'S
LITTLE INSTRUCTION BOOK

JASMINE BIRTLES

BOXTREE

First published in Great Britain in 1997 by
Boxtree Limited
an imprint of Macmillan Books, 25 Eccleston Place, London SW1W 9NF

10 9 8 7 6 5 4 3 2 1

ISBN: 0 7522 1107 2

Cover design: Shoot That Tiger!
Page design: Nigel Davies

Printed and bound in the United Kingdom byRedwood Books, Trowbridge, Wiltshire

A CIP catalogue entry for this book is available from the British Library.

Fatherhood. If you managed to be present at the birth that's more than some men, who can't even get their act together to be present at the conception. But more of Michael Jackson later. Fatherhood is a big responsibility, particularly if you are a male termite – if you mate with the queen termite you'll have about 40,000 offspring in the first week. Imagine the bill from the CSA! But fatherhood can also be fun and it's a great opportunity to be boss. After all, fathers always have the last words and those words are 'Ask your mother.'

Try to give your children everything
you never had as a child:
a mortgage, overdraft, hair-loss…

• • •

Save money at Christmas –
convert the whole family to Islam
a week beforehand.

Of course children need fathers –
no one else is so easy to ignore.

• • •

Children are a wonder of nature.
They're only a foot high but they can
still look down on their fathers.

To find your son's skateboard,
first try walking barefoot
round the house in the dark.

• • •

Modern toys are so complicated
only a child can use them.

A child is a creature that
stands between you
and Match Of The Day.

• • •

The more expensive the toy,
the more interest
the child will show in the box.

Never lend your car to anyone
who calls you father
(unless you're a priest).

• • •

A toddler can last for weeks without
going to the toilet but the moment you hit the road
he needs to go every five minutes.

If you want to stop your child
eating greasy, processed, unhealthy food,
don't let him eat off your plate.

• • •

Setting a good example for your children
takes all the fun out of manhood.

If you want a child to do something
for you suggest it just before bedtime.

• • •

Definition of irritation:
raising your children under the eyes
of your parents.

To avoid making the same mistakes
as your parents,
get busy creating your own ones.

• • •

The best part of fatherhood is
the pain and suffering of childbirth –
undertaken by somebody else.

Save money on kids –
get a dog instead.

• • •

Remember when you used to look
forward to school holidays?

Men who use the rhythm method
are called fathers.

• • •

Remember, children in the front seat
can cause accidents.
Accidents in the back seat can cause children.

A new baby is like a second-hand car:
it comes complete with two-lung power,
toxic emissions, disposable seat-covers
and an easily-flooded carburettor.

• • •

Educate your child.
Smash his computer.

You know you're a new man if you
can change a nappy without having
to brag about it down the pub.

• • •

How to lose pounds quickly: be around
when your teenager is about to go out.

To keep your marriage going have
separate holidays – yours and the children's.

• • •

Don't worry, nappy changing doesn't go on for
ever, it just seems like it.

Having a baby adds to your relationship
with your partner – it gives you
something entirely new to argue about.

• • •

Fathers always have the last words in any
family and those words are 'Ask your mother'.

Fathers of teenagers should
never admit to knowing about sex,
drugs, money problems or fashion.
Every teenager knows that he's the only one
who understands them – that's his job.

The worst kind of father is one
who gets so excited at the birth
of his child that he immediately
rushes out to tell all his friends –
and never comes back.

Babies' cries are like police sirens.
They wake the neighbours, make
your heart sink and everyone else
disappears at the sound.

• • •

Desensitise your baby to noise.
Learn to drill roads at home.

Things that send a baby to sleep:
driving round in a car, being sung to,
listening to a vacuum cleaner and being
told about your birdie on the 16th hole.

• • •

Children go free on holiday –
that's because it's not a holiday.

If it moves, opens or shifts
in any way, fit a childlock.
That goes for your mouth too.

• • •

Definition of a mother-in-law:
the backseat driver in the motorcar
of child-rearing.

Children should be seen
and not heard. Teenagers
are only seen in a herd.

• • •

A child is a cuddly,
sweet-looking money pit.

Driving rules:

1) A child in a car will always have the sun in its eyes

2) A child will only be sick in a new car

3) 'Are we there yet?' means you're five minutes off a traffic jam and a lost temper.

Having a child means you'll have
someone to beat at chess –
if only for the next 5 years.

• • •

Children ignore anything
they can't dismantle or eat.

If you want your
child's attention, start a fight.

• • •

A father has traditionally had only
a small part to play in family life –
particularly if he plays golf.

If you haven't got carried away
as a father, you should be.

• • •

Teenagers don't like doing homework.
To them, work is an invasion of privacy.

At school, your son is known
by the company he avoids.

• • •

Your teenage daughter is known
by the company she doesn't avoid.

One father is worth
100 schoolteachers.

• • •

'Homework' is work
that kids leave at home.

Marriage is an institution.
Children are dad's destitution.

• • •

Prepare your children for
the real world – tell them
their pocket money is a loan.

Mother's ruin is
when father ran.

• • •

You can't expect your son to be
a true bully until you've sent him
to a good school.

One problem with having children
is that they eventually become
old enough to make you presents
at school – like a pipe rack for
their non-smoking dad.

It's a wise father that knows when
to keep out of his son's bedroom.

• • •

Daddy's little girl is also
daddy's little debt.

Marriage is a contract:
parenthood is two sleeping partners.

• • •

A daughter is a daughter until she's married.
A son is a son until he wrecks your car.

The joy of fatherhood is best seen
in the relieved smile of your own father.

• • •

The greatest form of contraception is a child –
in your bedroom.

Three stages of fatherhood:
pride, perseverance, poverty.

• • •

If faced with fatherhood or joining the Mafia,
choose the Mafia. The hours are better
and you get to wear smarter clothes.

Warning: babies come
with a yell-by date.

• • •

Treat your baby like a china cup.
Hold it gently, admire the design
and always put the milk in first.

The school run is a chance to show off
your pride and joy – the car.

• • •

Teach your son the facts of life:
the birds, the bees and the bills.

A child only remembers Father's Day
with gentle prompting. Try a banner.

• • •

Children don't ask to be born but
they will be asked to mow the lawn.

One child is a joy, two are a trial,
three is just asking for trouble.

• • •

If your home is tidy, your sleep is regular
and love-life satisfactory,
why not ruin it all and become a father?

Every child is a genius until it
discovers chocolate and mud.

• • •

Confuse your teenager. Come home
at a ridiculous hour, whinge at your wife
and treat the place like a hotel.

To err is human…
and fatherly.

• • •

The best way to keep your word to your
children is not to give it in the first place.

No father with any pride
will attempt to dance.

• • •

There are two kinds of travel –
first class and with children.

If your teenage son wants to
learn to drive, don't stand in his way.

• • •

You know you love your son if he has
every toy you ever wanted.

Outings with children consist
of trips from toilet to toilet.

• • •

Save money on Christmas presents –
smash the TV in October.

You ought to worry when…
your teenager's bedroom is tidy.

• • •

If your child brings back something
he's made for you at school, he's probably
softening the blow of the report card.

Teenage girls are physically unable to
communicate except by phone.

• • •

You know you're past it when
your child comes home with homework
in which you can't help them to cheat.

All teenagers are selectively deaf.
They are congenitally unable to hear
words like 'work', 'wash' and 'get up'
but can hear the word 'party'
at any volume.

Develop a mad act. Talk to yourself loudly on occasions, wear a tea-cosy on Sundays or anything else that takes your fancy. It'll keep your children amused when they're small and will stop them bringing their friends into the house when they're older.

It's not easy being a father.
If it were, more of them would stick around.

• • •

You know your child has grown up
when he utters the magic words
'What would you like to drink Dad?'

A teenager's true home is
where they send the bills.

• • •

If you want to keep your children on
the straight and narrow take them bowling –
it gets them off the streets and into the alleys.

Be master of your own home –
live in the shed.

• • •

Don't worry that your children
never listen to you, just worry that
they are always copying you.

By the time a father thinks his family
can make ends meet, someone moves the ends.

• • •

When you return from holiday…
is when you need a holiday.

The best way to keep your teenagers
at home is to take an interest
in their activities, be understanding
of their problems and hide
the keys to the car.

Fathers shouldn't worry about
being up-to-date with youth culture
because when you think about it,
youth culture is a contradiction
in terms anyway.

To heir is human.

• • •

Teach your children not to steal from school.
After all, you can bring them all the stationery
they need from work.

Fatherhood is the greatest single
preserve of the amateur.

• • •

You know you're an overprotective father if you
won't let your child play near the toy train tracks.

Children have wonderful imaginations.
They can even imagine
that you're a great father.

• • •

In a child's world, 'competition' is
an inter-schools football game, 'responsibility'
is a paper round and a 'VIP' is his dad.

Children are great mimics.
They'll act like you do however much
you try to teach them good manners.

• • •

If your parents come to stay your wife
might bake a cake. If your in-laws come
to stay you should fake an ache.

Never ask your partner if
she's pregnant unless you're certain she is.

• • •

Although children are great mimics,
they never try to imitate anyone tidy.

If you must be an example to your child be an example of how not to conduct your life.

• • •

Never put off till tomorrow what you could con your children into doing for you today.

Get your child used to hand-me-downs.
Clothes, toys, your overdraft...

• • •

Children are supposed to look after you in
your old age, so why not retire now?

Bees make honey, birds make nests,
children make mess.

• • •

A father is like a priest – always ready
to hear a confession and usually celibate.

Follow the advice on medicine bottles:
'Keep Away From Children'.

• • •

One thing worse than a poorly child:
a poorly father.

Out of the mouths of babes...
come huge dry-cleaning bills.

• • •

Children help you exercise...
your patience.

A child changes everything –
mostly sleep patterns.

• • •

The only certain way to
silence a child is bribery.

A silent child means
something is broken.

• • •

Encourage your child to make his own
entertainment – but not with your credit card.

'Baby changing facilities' doesn't mean
you can swop yours for another one.

• • •

Remember when 'playing with an activitity
centre' was something you did with your wife?

Don't have a child, have a giraffe.
Half an hour after birth they are
up and able to feed themselves,
and they never make a fuss
in Toys 'R' Us.

You know you're a father when:
1) Your video collection is all cartoons
2) Interior decorating means covering up
the crayon marks
3) The only paintings you own are made
out of pasta and stuck on the fridge.

If your children nag you to get them a dog buy a dachshund – they're already stretched to their limit and can't be harmed any more by children pulling at each end.

Patience is a vir…
will you be quiet!?!

• • •

Enjoy your child's first words,
because from now on it's a sentence.

Fathers are made out of money –
thin, papery and easily spent.

• • •

You're only young once, but if you
become a dad you can be immature for ever.

Raising a child is like running a marathon.
A lot of tiring work and only a blanket at the end.

• • •

If you want a stable family life,
bring up horses.

If you've gone for a trophy wife you could
end up with consolation prize kids.

• • •

Teach your kids the value of money.
Tax their pocket money.

Crash course in child development:
show them how to use the remote control.

• • •

You have to make allowances for your
teenagers, and as far as they're concerned,
the bigger the better.

Pretend to be a cowboy,
have your children seen and herded.

• • •

Make your teenagers pay their
telephone bills, then they'll work
their fingers to the phone.

Curse of the Mummy – what happens
when you say 'yes' after their mum said 'no'.

• • •

Some men actually accept sleep deprivation
torture – it's called fathering.

Help your children understand the value
of money – charge things to their credit cards.

• • •

If you want to teach your son how to
treat girls, lie about your past.

Teach your teenagers to drive only
if they've bought the car.

• • •

If you're having less fun in bed with your partner
now it could be because something's between you
– like the baby.

When you became a father you traded
the call of the wild for the crawl of the child.

• • •

You know your children are growing up
if they stop wanting their questions answered
and you just get your answers questioned.

Learn to laugh at yourself. After all,
you don't want to be the last one to get the joke.

• • •

Try and give your children everything
you didn't have as a boy – computer games,
mobile phones, friends…

The best cure for car sickness –
don't let your kids drive it.

• • •

Fathers are best at being understanding
when their sons go through that
difficult age – 13 to 53.

If you're a new father you
probably can't remember a time when
an alarm clock was a small instrument
at the side of your bed rather than
a large wail from the bed at your side.

Fathers today aren't necessarily
the ones that wear the trousers
at home but just you see
what happens if you suggest that
you wear the dresses…!

You're a family man if the money
in your wallet has all been replaced by photos.

• • •

Love thy neighbours:
then they're more likely to babysit.

Family ties are what the in-laws
always buy you for Christmas.

• • •

An even-tempered father is one
who is always grumpy.

Combine fatherly advice
with practical solutions.
For example, 'it's a jungle
out there, so go
and mow the lawn'.

The grass is always greener
on the other side of the fence
because your neighbour
never returns your
borrowed gardening tools.

Fatherly love: the ability to expect
the best from your children, despite the facts.

• • •

Fatherhood –
the one you wear when it's raining.

If you're thinking of becoming a father,
get a job and practise growling.

• • •

Fathers are like bread rolls:
crusty on the outside, soft on the inside
and past their best by midday.

Carry your children when they're young
in the hope they'll carry you when you're old.

• • •

A father's solemn duty is to take
his children to football matches and
teach them what to shout at the ref.

Bored games
lead to board games.

• • •

Fathers need to let their children win at sports
sometimes. If you haven't lost at tiddlywinks
you're not a proper dad.

Fathers are best at loving the kids when
mum is busy doing the housework.

• • •

Dads may be the leader of the pack
but more often they're the joker.

Fathers are best at being strong and clever
and mothers are best at telling them they are.

• • •

Father knows best, which is why he always
has the TV remote control.

The best reason to be a father:
unlimited chances to play with train sets.

• • •

Empathise with your pregnant wife.
Get a beer belly.

Screaming and crying are quite natural. But sometimes you can let the baby do it too.

• • •

Of course your child loves you.
All children love clowns.

Nature is wonderful –
women get to have the babies
and fathers get to spout off
in the pub about how it's
revolutionised their lives.

Fathers are usually the breadwinners, but as far as children are concerned the proper ones are also the cake and ice-cream winners.

When you were a bachelor
you could spend weekend mornings
lying in bed wondering when to get up.
Now you're a father you're up
hours before morning wondering
when you can get to bed.

Before you were a dad
babysitters only ever
appeared in sitcoms,
now they turn your
home into one.

A law of baby comedy:
if a joke is good
it's worth repeating,
over and over and over again...
particularly if it's peek-a-boo.

If you spend too much time
with kids your brain
goes to jelly. If you even know
what flavour it is
you're really in trouble.

Pregnancy – a time when
men have to deal with
mood swings, food cravings
and being told to snap out of it
by their pregnant partner.

Pregnancy – a time when
you realise just how
pointless a man's existence is
in the grand scheme of things.

The arrival of a baby is the
biggest chance a man gets to grow up.
It is usually the one time in his life
that he realises he will never again
be the centre of attention.

When you are a father you learn
what women have known all along –
that success comes from
muddling through, coping with mess
and never being fazed by stickiness.

Try to resist the urge to refer
to your baby in derogatory terms.
Names like Maggot, Wriggly Worm
and Anklebiter will not go down well
with your partner.

Remember, your partner does need you to stick around once the child is born. Women need something to complain about – that's what you are there for.

Baby feeding law:
for every one mouthful
that goes in her mouth,
at least six will
end up elsewhere.

A father's main function
is to buy the expensive
shoes their little girl
wanted that mummy
wouldn't buy.

When going on trips, babies really
need a mother, a father and an experienced valet.

• • •

Once your first child arrives you can
never press the 'pause' button again –
everything goes into 'fast-forward'.

A child is like a new sport, exhilarating, tiring and you'll need lots of expensive equipment.

• • •

When in company, fatherly affection should be either unashamedly ostentatious or not visible at all.

Being the father of a toddler
is like being a film star's agent –
you need to guide him in the
right direction, massage his ego
and stop him stuffing
unhealthy things up his nose.

The 'terrible twos' are what happens
when baby misses the potty again.

• • •

Watch what you say to your toddler.
He may get as far as school-age thinking
his name is 'Behave'.

Make sure your child gets lots of fresh air –
put the TV in the garden.

• • •

Teach your children not to be afraid of the Devil.
Tell them he's just like Father Christmas –
daddy in disguise.

Definition of a playful toddler:
a groin-seeking missile.

• • •

With teenagers it is better to give than
to receive – especially if it is a call from
the next county asking for a lift home.

One good turn gets
most of the duvet.

• • •

Giving your student offspring money is bad
for their health – it brings on amnesia.

Teenage logic: 'I can't be poor,
Dad's still got a cheque book.'

• • •

You know you're overweight when your kids
use you as a bouncy castle.

If your children go off the rails it could
be because you made the wrong mistakes.

• • •

Whatever age your child is people will
tell you its 'the best age' – unless it's
more than 12, then they go all quiet.

It's not necessary to bring your golf clubs
when participating in the school sports day.

• • •

When you have to discuss the facts of life
with your children don't be nervous –
they'll explain it all very clearly for you.

Avoid meal-time hassles with children
by feeding them nothing but chocolate.

• • •

Avoid paying for expensive child car seats
by leaving your kids at home.

A child is a drain on resources and
your resources down the drain.

• • •

Be sympathetic during childbirth.
Your pain will start soon enough.

Good children always forgive you
when they're wrong.

• • •

Half the fun of fatherhood
is getting there.

It's not what
your daughter knows
that should bother you,
it's how she found out.

Jasmine Birtles is a registered trademark of The Sonyoung Electronics Corporation of Merthyr Tydfil. In 1992, she was merged with their publication division, slimmed down, rationalised and downsized. She is now a world-renowned authority on anything she can get paid for. She knows about fatherhood having been school bully as a child. She took a delight in pulling other kids' hair and stamping on their glasses: her mother was a hairdresser and her father an optician. Later in life she became an academic and wrote her doctoral thesis on slugs. Sadly a lot of them got killed going through the printer. She has been married and divorced 68 times and now lives in a shoe box on the A30.